Meet the Stars
of
Dawson's Creek

Meet the Stars of Dawson's Creek

Grace Catalano

LAUREL-LEAF BOOKS

Published by
Bantam Doubleday Dell Books for Young Readers
a division of
Bantam Doubleday Dell Publishing Group, Inc.
1540 Broadway
New York, New York 10036

The trademark Laurel-Leaf Library® is registered in the
U.S. Patent and Trademark Office.
The trademark Dell® is registered in the U.S. Patent and
Trademark Office.
ISBN 0-440-22821-2

Printed in the United States of America
June 1998
10 9 8 7 6 5 4 3
OPM

For Rosemarie Catalano
(a.k.a. Mom)
You've been there with me
through teen TV
past and present

Contents

Acknowledgments

The author would like to thank Joseph Catalano and Phil Berry for help shaping this book. To Rose Miele, Sam Alan, and my dad, Salvatore Catalano, for their endless patience and support. Thanks also to Grace Palazzo, Ralph J. Miele, Mary Michaels, and Jane Burns.

And special thanks to Beverly Horowitz, Karen Meyers, and everyone who worked on this book at Bantam Doubleday Dell.

Meet the Stars
of
Dawson's Creek

Welcome to Awesome Dawson's Creek

Since its debut on Tuesday, January 20, 1998, *Dawson's Creek* has become the most talked-about new show on television. *Dawson's Creek* has taken America by Storm.

In its first four weeks on the air, the show received a 5.2 Nielsen rating, reaching more than five million homes. According to the ratings, *Dawson's Creek* is the number one show among girls twelve to seventeen and number four among teens overall. It is currently the WB's highest-rated show, ahead of the popular *Buffy the Vampire Slayer,* which is *Dawson's* lead-in on Tuesday night.

What are the secret ingredients that make *Dawson's Creek* stand out? Why has it become a hit in such a short time? Perhaps the appeal of *Dawson's Creek* can be summed up by Kevin Williamson, the show's creator-producer, who is also famous as the writer behind *Scream* and *Scream 2*. He says, "I think it's [the show is] truthful. There's nothing preachy about it. The moment anyone says anything that sounds like a message, the characters discard it. They go, 'So what did we learn from this *90210* moment?'"

That may be one of the attractions, but the main reason for tuning in is to catch up with the show's four gorgeous headliners. Almost overnight, *Dawson's Creek* has transformed a quartet of relatively anonymous young actors into stars. James Van Der Beek (Dawson Leery), Joshua Jackson (Pacey Witter), Michelle Williams (Jennifer Lindley), and Katie Holmes (Joey Potter) have slipped into their roles with such ease and style that it seems as if they were born to play them. Their chemistry is explosive, their timing is terrific, and their appeal is sensational.

Just one month after the show's debut, these four fresh faces began gracing the covers of magazines like *Seventeen, YM,* and *Teen. TV Guide* dedicated a separate collectible cover to each of the hot young stars—and the magazines flew off the shelves. Fans of the show have now become fans of its stars. They can't get enough of this fab foursome!

It seems as if everyone is asking the same questions. Who are these young actors? Where did they come from? What are they really like? This books covers the very private lives of TV's hottest four new stars—so sit back and enjoy!

Putting It Together

Kevin Williamson deserves all the credit for getting *Dawson's Creek* on the air. The hot screenwriter of the hit teen horror flicks *Scream, Scream 2,* and *I Know What You Did Last Summer* created *Dawson's Creek* and fought to have his sophisticated show produced.

Dawson's Creek has been called a contemporary *Catcher in the Rye*. It's been called a combination of *Beverly Hills 90210* and *Party of Five*. But *Dawson's Creek* is totally original.

Set in a quiet, picturesque New England town called Capeside, the show revolves around the lives of three close friends: budding filmmaker Dawson Leery (James Van Der Beek), sarcastic tomboy Josephine "Joey" Potter (Katie Holmes), and class clown Pacey

Witter (Joshua Jackson). Their friendship is interrupted by the arrival of a mysterious girl from New York City, Jennifer Lindley (Michelle Williams).

The show has been hailed for its snappy dialogue and realistic depiction of teenage life. While the people behind it may have learned from the success of shows like *Beverly Hills 90210* and *Party of Five, Dawson's Creek* goes to a whole new level. *Dawson's Creek* is fresh, funny, sexy, and *real.* Joshua Jackson calls it "a mouthpiece for real teens."

Michelle Williams explains, "The sense of reality is really very grounded. Like the emotions, fears, and joys are exactly what I went through in high school. That's what really attracted me to the show, is how honest it is. This is the kind of show that everyone should be watching and paying attention to."

One of the reasons the audience can so easily relate to Kevin Williamson's characters is that they aren't necessarily the coolest kids in school. "I take the kids who are basically immature," says Williamson, "and turn them into the responsible ones."

James Van Der Beek feels that this is one of the reasons why *Dawson's Creek* has become so popular so fast. "I call Dawson the dork in all of us," says the actor. "He's not really, really cool, and he's not part of the 'in' crowd. He's, you know, different. And I think a lot of the things he goes through are very universal."

Williamson originally developed *Dawson's Creek* for the Fox network, which had super success with teen-oriented shows like *Beverly Hills 90210* and *Party of Five*. He pitched the story to Fox in 1994. Fox seriously considered adding *Dawson's Creek* to its lineup, but thought it was too similar to the then struggling *Party of Five*. Fox passed on it, and Warner Brothers executives grabbed it during the summer of 1996.

Ironically, three of the guiding forces behind *Dawson's Creek* were former Fox executives. Jamie Kellner, now chief executive of the WB, was a former Fox executive who had a hand in the success of shows like *Married . . . With Children* and *Melrose Place*. *Dawson's Creek*'s executive producers Charles Rosin and Paul G. Stupin were both partly responsible for the success of *Beverly Hills 90210*.

Even though the fledgling WB isn't yet established as a major player in the television game, Williamson was happy just to have his show on the air. He was assured that the WB would give the show a chance at success, the same way Fox had with *Party of Five*. Williamson was well aware of the fact that a bigger network might cancel his show if the ratings weren't as high as expected. It had already happened with the critically acclaimed *My So-Called Life,* which was canceled by ABC before it had a chance to draw a big enough audience. Williamson didn't want that to happen to *Dawson's Creek*. It was just too personal to him.

Dawson's Creek is based on Kevin Williamson's own adolescent memories. Born in New Bern, North Carolina, he knows what it's like to live in a small town and dream of bigger things. Like Dawson, Williamson was completely obsessed with movies and directors like Steven Spielberg. Growing up, Williamson knew most of the lines from Spielberg's film *Jaws* by heart. In fact, when he was just a teenager Williamson encouraged his librarian to order a subscription to the entertainment industry's daily magazine, *Variety*.

Williamson says he bases most of *Dawson's Creek*'s plots on fact. When he came under fire for the show's most controversial story line—Pacey's affair with his teacher—Williamson reported that a teacher at his high school did, in fact, have an affair with a student.

Like the characters on *Dawson's Creek*, Williamson grew up near an inlet. He sailed across it to visit his friend Fannie Norwood, on whom the character Joey is based.

"There are a lot of hidden memories in the show," says Williamson. "If Fannie watches, she will know exactly where I got some stuff. It's nice because only she will know.

"I remember the first time someone made my heart flutter," he continues. "I remember the first time my knees got weak. And that's what the show is about."

The real *Dawson's Creek* is only a few miles away from Williamson's childhood home. His adolescent years were spent in Oriental, North Carolina, where his father, Wade, a fisherman, and mother, Faye, still reside.

Williamson studied theater and film at East Carolina University before moving to New York in 1987 to try to break into acting. When the only acting jobs that came his way were bit parts on the soap opera *Another World,* Williamson knew he had to find another profession.

He decided to try his luck on the other side of the camera, as a writer and director. He packed his bags and moved to Los Angeles in 1991. "When I got there, I just soaked it up," he remembers. "The first day I went to Universal Studios and saw Bruce the shark (from *Jaws*). I had to because that whole Spielberg thing I have is real."

While working as an assistant to a music video director, Williamson began writing scripts in his spare time. His childhood fascination with horror movies led him to create the screenplay for *Scream*. The film, directed by legendary horror director Wes Craven, was a hit at the box office, turned Williamson into an overnight celebrity, and revived the teen horror genre. Williamson's follow-ups to *Scream* were its sequel, *Scream 2,* and *I Know What You Did Last Summer,* based on the classic novel by Lois Duncan.

He's now developing another TV series called *WasteLAnd*. "The show is simple," he says. "Take these *Dawson's* kids, age them by eight years, and move them to L.A. without a clue." He is also working on the script for

Scream 3 and will direct his first feature, *Killing Mrs. Tingle,* about a group of high-school students who plan to murder their teacher.

One thing can be said of Kevin Williamson: He knows how to cast his projects. His films have starred the hottest young actors in Hollywood, including *Party of Five*'s Neve Campbell and Jennifer Love Hewitt, *Friends* star Courteney Cox, Sarah Michelle Gellar from *Buffy the Vampire Slayer,* and Skeet Ulrich and Jerry O'Connell, to name just a few.

When the time came to cast *Dawson's Creek,* Williamson looked for unknown actors who would be able to breathe life into his characters. He and the casting directors auditioned scores of young hopefuls for the four pivotal roles. They were searching for the special qualities they knew would send *Dawson's Creek* over the top. And they were immediately impressed with the four actors who would eventually win the parts.

The show was cast, the first few scripts were written, and shooting was scheduled to begin in May 1997 at the studios in Wilmington, North Carolina. Everything seemed to be falling smoothly into place.

The series' creative team had great confidence in what they were doing, even though they knew the show would create a certain amount of controversy. But when the new shows for the fall 1997 season were announced, *Dawson's Creek* was not one of them. Even though the pilot had been shot, the WB's marketing department was still working on a media blitz for the new show. The marketers weren't about to throw *Dawson's Creek* on TV in September with every other new series—without any fanfare.

The WB had so much faith in the series, it backed the show with a $3-million marketing campaign. *Dawson's Creek* started generating word of mouth months before it hit the air. The marketing blitz included trailers in theaters, posters on buses, and billboards at major intersections. The official wardrobe provider, J. Crew, featured the then unknown cast in its winter-spring 1997 catalog.

By January 1998, the WB had promos of the show running in Blockbuster video stores with Paula Cole's song "I Don't Want to Wait" as its soundtrack. With everyone already thinking the song was the *Dawson's Creek* theme, Paula gave permission to the producers to use it for the show's title sequence. Since then, hot music by artists like Beth Nielsen Chapman, Jewel, No Doubt, and Sheryl Crow has been heard on the show. Already, a soundtrack CD is in the works.

By the fall of 1997, the WB was only three years old and broadcasting just nine hours a week in prime time. The WB had no real breakout hit show and, as a startup network, was consistently losing money.

In television circles, the WB was being written off as a new network that had tried and failed. That is, until the fall of 1997, when *Buffy the Vampire Slayer* debuted. With a cast of fresh, young stars, *Buffy* became the WB's highest-rated Monday-night show.

Encouraged by its success with *Buffy,* the WB announced that *Dawson's Creek* would debut on Tuesday, January 20, in the eight-to-nine-P.M. slot. When some TV critics griped at the news that the new show would air during that family hour, the WB decided to move it to the nine-to-ten-P.M. slot. The network then moved *Buffy,* its strongest show at the time, from Monday to Tuesday night at eight P.M. as *Dawson's Creek*'s lead-in.

The decision was a good one. According to Kevin Williamson, "the nine o'clock time gives me more freedom. I don't want to be limited in what I can do."

No one had any idea how long it would take for *Dawson's Creek* to catch on. Television viewers today have more than a hundred channels to choose from at any given time. Despite polls, surveys, and other tests, picking a successful TV show is a toss-up—at best a guess about what viewers will want to watch. In the history of television no one has been able to predict what will be a hit show and what will fail.

When *Dawson's Creek* hit the airwaves, it received mixed reviews, but most critics praised it and called it the most irresistible new show of the year. The critics who were less than enthusiastic believed that the show's open discussion of teen sex would lead to its extinction. But that has only added to the show's appeal. It took just a few episodes, some major raves from top national newspapers and magazines, and a little publicity to get audiences interested.

At first the audience attention was barely perceptible. Some letters came in from fans, mostly teenagers, who were writing to one or all of the show's four stars. Little by little, mail began to pour into the WB offices.

By the beginning of March 1998, the verdict was in. *Dawson's Creek* had beaten *Buffy the Vampire Slayer* in ratings and was the highest-rated show in WB history. *Buffy the Vampire Slayer* is hot, but *Dawson's Creek* is hotter!

James Van Der Beek

*D*espite playing the role of Dawson Leery, the blond heartthrob of *Dawson's Creek*, James Van Der Beek doesn't think of himself as a star. The notion of fame is so far from James's mind that he's still surprised when people recognize him. He hasn't yet come to terms with the idea that he is on a fast track to stardom and there's no turning back.

When *Dawson's Creek* was first beginning to catch on and James's face started popping up on the covers of magazines, he was asked what it felt like to be an idol. His reply: "They tell me I have to be completely ready for this. But I have no idea what to expect."

For James, life hasn't changed that much. Even though the twenty-one-year-old actor is on one of the hottest shows on TV, he still lives a quiet life. In fact, just before he started playing Dawson, he was attending Drew University in Madison, New Jersey. James, a dean's list student, received an academic scholarship and was majoring in English with a minor in sociology. He signed up for a leave of absence from college to work on the show.

James Van Der Beek, Jr., was born on March 8, 1977, in Cheshire, Connecticut. He's the oldest of three children. His dad, James senior, is a cellular phone company executive, and his mom, Melinda, runs a gymnastics studio. His mother says James was an adorable baby who looked at the world with big, beautiful eyes and never stopped smiling.

James's first interest was sports. In school, he was on the football team and thought for a while that he would eventually play the sport professionally.

He was a natural athlete, endowed with strength and coordination. James is the kind of guy who believes that if you're going to do something, you should put all your energy into it and do it really well. Football became a great outlet for him. He had an overabundance of energy and put it all into playing the rough and aggressive game. His quickness and fired-up enthusiasm for football turned him into what he describes as a "big sports person."

Then, as fast as football had entered his life, it was cut off. When James was thirteen years old, he suffered a mild concussion and wasn't allowed to play on the football team that year. Needing a place to channel his energy, he decided to try out for the school play. He had never thought about acting before. The only other acting he had done to that point was a fifth-grade play about the Declaration of Independence.

Nonetheless, James landed the lead role of Danny Zuko in the school's production of *Grease*. It was his first taste of acting, and it changed his life forever.

James had a blast onstage playing the role that John Travolta made famous on the big screen. He hadn't taken any formal lessons in singing, acting, or dancing, but picked up on performing very quickly. From the time he first stepped onto the stage, he knew it was something he wanted to keep doing.

"I really like to act," he confides today. "I went into it and stuck with it because I really do enjoy it, not because I was hoping to become a famous star."

He did, however, enjoy the new recognition he received in school, especially from girls. Starring in *Grease,* James felt not only truly accepted by his peers for the first time, but admired by them as well. "All of a sudden I felt like I knew what I was doing," he remembers. "And I got all this attention."

After *Grease,* James told his parents he wanted to continue acting. At first his mother wasn't sure it was a good idea. She wanted her son to enjoy a normal, happy adolescence. She knew the competition would be rough and that dozens of aspiring actors fail for every one who succeeds. At age thirteen, his mother felt, James was too young to experience rejection.

But James couldn't get acting out of his mind. He saw no reason why he shouldn't at least give it a try.

For the next three years, James auditioned for countless roles at the Cheshire Theater Ensemble. With his undeniable natural talent and charm, the young, bright-eyed boy won nearly every role he tried out for.

James also began extensive dance and voice training with the Connecticut Academy of Performing Arts. He was able to juggle all this with his studies, maintaining a straight-A average and winning an academic scholarship to the prestigious Cheshire Academy, a private school founded in 1794.

James finally decided, at age sixteen, to ask his mom if he could audition for a professional acting job. When she agreed to drive him into New York City, he stared at her in disbelief. Today, he says, "I think she secretly wanted me to go in and see what a terrible business acting was and to decide that this really wasn't what I wanted to do."

James's mother sat him down and laid out some very definite guidelines. " 'I'll give you the summer to make the rounds and see if you could get an agent and get your foot in the door' was how she put it," he says.

To James and his mother's surprise, he landed both an agent and a manager on their very first visit to New York. But before he won any acting jobs, James would have to go on auditions.

James had two things going for him. The first was his great looks—blond, boyish, and preppie. He also had a résumé with range. He had already played a variety of roles: Matt in *The Fantasticks*, Lamar/Jeffrey in *Godspell,* the Scarecrow in *The Wizard of Oz,* and Andy Lee in *42nd Street.*

His agent began sending James on auditions for television commercials. He was assured that all young actors begin their careers in commercials, and everyone hoped he wouldn't have any problem getting a job. But he soon found out it wasn't as easy as he'd thought.

To everyone's disappointment, he had no success auditioning for commercials. The unknown teenage actor began to learn the rejection that many must face in show business. Deep down inside, James really didn't expect to start working as an actor right away. He was realistic about the business, and with the love, guidance, and support of his parents, he was able to handle all the pressures he found himself under.

He kept auditioning. Almost every day the young hopeful would climb into his mother's car, and together they would drive to interviews and tryouts. James found he had to forget about sports and most after-school activities. Sometimes he felt like giving up. He would sit in waiting rooms and think of going home to rest and study for school.

But he kept trying. The rejections made him realize how much harder he had to work to achieve his goal. "I honestly believe that there is more rejection in acting than in any other field," he says.

He admits that if his mother hadn't been there to guide him through the disappointment, he never would have had the patience to continue his climb up the ladder. "I owe it all to my mom," he says. "It really would have been impossible without her support."

Finally James began to have some success in his auditions. "I knew there was going to be a lot of rejection associated with auditioning, but I didn't get anything for a year," he says. "Then, once I figured out how to give the best audition, I became the callback king."

His method was simple: reexamine, develop, and perfect his style of auditioning. "After that, casting agents would call my agent and say, 'Where did you find him? He's great,'" says James. "But I still didn't get the part."

Eventually he did get called back and cast. The first role he won was a spot on *The Red Booth Christmas Special* on ABC, followed by a guest-starring role on an episode of

Nickelodeon's *Clarissa Explains It All,* which starred Melissa Joan Hart, now star of ABC's *Sabrina, the Teenage Witch.*

Next James was sent on an audition for a stage play. It was an off-Broadway production of *Finding the Sun,* written and directed by Pulitzer prize–winning playwright Edward Albee. James won the role of Fergus. "I played a very idealized version of Edward at sixteen," he says.

James describes this as the defining moment for him as an actor. He and his mother drove into Manhattan every day over the play's three-month run. He kept up with his schoolwork during the day and appeared in the play at night. On matinee days, he did two shows.

Of his theater experience, James says, "I love the theater because I can try different things every night."

When *Finding the Sun* ended, James's agent had him audition for a role in the twentieth-anniversary production of *Shenandoah* at the Goodspeed Opera House in East Haddam, Connecticut. The original musical, which won two Tony awards, began its life during the summer of 1974 at the Goodspeed Opera House, where many Broadway-bound hits and revivals are born or born again.

James craved a role in the twentieth-anniversary production. The auditions were held in New York and involved reading, singing, and dancing. On the day of his first audition, James won the part of Henry Anderson based on his looks. But then a serious throat problem made him unable to talk, much less sing, so, a few days later, he was forced to go to an open call for the show.

At the time James didn't have his Actors' Equity card (he got it at the end of his run in *Shenandoah*). A guy at the stage door told James to come back when the Equity performers had finished auditioning.

"The only reason they saw me was because my agent set up an appointment for me before," says James. During the tryout, he did something he had never done before. Because *Shenandoah* is such a sentimental family story, he says, "During the read-through, I had tears in my eyes . . . and I never cry."

After a series of callbacks, James found himself up against five other young hopefuls. Finally he got the good news: He had won the part of Henry Anderson.

Based on the 1965 James Stewart movie of the same name, *Shenandoah* tells the story of Charlie Anderson, a Virginia widower, who refuses to let his sons enlist in the Confederate Army or become involved in the Civil War.

James played one of the sons and says his part had little dialogue, but he did get the chance to sing and dance. His favorite part of the show was performing the rousing number "Next to Lovin' (I Like Fightin')" with Marc Kudisch, Bill Whitefield, Michael Park, and James Ludwig, who played the other Anderson sons.

James says, "If you were to look at the script in the beginning, my character wasn't that big. My job as an actor was to figure out where my character fit into the family, what he thought and how he reacted. Once I did that, I had to make him different from all the other brothers, so that the audience would know who Henry was and feel his reactions throughout the story." The cast also had a voice coach backstage because they all had to learn a Virginian drawl, which James referred to as a "twangy sort of accent."

Shenandoah played at the Goodspeed Opera House from July 6 to September 30, 1994. Even though the theater was not far from James's hometown of Cheshire, he decided to live away from home for the summer. He and the actors in the show lived in houses owned by the Goodspeed. James went home to Cheshire on his days off.

James got along well with the other actors in *Shenandoah* but remembers the production as a lot of hard work. "Things are not as wild or as crazy as some people might expect from a bunch of theater people," he explains. "With so many matinee days—three a week—we couldn't afford to be that crazy, or that stupid, because the show would have suffered."

James felt right at home on the stage of the Goodspeed Opera House during the summer of 1994. He called it the "best lifestyle there is and the best summer of my life." The cast lovingly dubbed their headquarters Camp Goodspeed because they had such an enjoyable time there.

When *Shenandoah* closed in September 1994, James returned home for his senior year at Cheshire Academy. He maintained an A average despite dozens of New York auditions and missed school days.

He credits his success in school to the support he received from teachers. "Everyone was very patient and supportive of everything I did," he says. "Concerning my studies, they always let me know what I had to do, then let me make it up when I had to go into New York and couldn't take a test or final exam. I taught myself everything I could, just so I could stay on top of things."

As far as his career was concerned, James was being encouraged to think about singing professionally. But he disregarded that idea. He wanted to concentrate on acting.

The year 1995 was a turning point for James. He graduated from Cheshire Academy with high honors and began his freshman term at Drew University in Madison, New Jersey. He also got the biggest break of his career, winning the role of Rick Sanford in the feature film *Angus*.

Angus is a comedy about an overweight high-school boy, Angus Bethune (played by Charles Talbert), who secretly loves a popular, pretty girl who doesn't seem to know he exists. Ariana Richards plays Melissa, the object of Angus's affection. But Melissa only has eyes for arrogant jock Rick Sanford (played by James).

Angus gave James the chance to work with veteran actors Kathy Bates and George C.

Scott. "I couldn't believe it when they told me I was going to meet them," he says.

He also got along great with Ariana, who was in *Jurassic Park*, too. James asked Ariana many questions about her experience working on that movie and with Steven Spielberg. Ironically, he would soon be cast as Dawson Leery, whose idol is the famous director.

James's role in *Angus* finally gave him the recognition he deserved. Not only was his performance singled out in reviews of the film, but producers and casting directors were starting to become more familiar with him and his work. And it wasn't long after *Angus* that *Dawson's Creek* came along.

James was sent on the audition for *Dawson's* but never thought it would be the role that would change his life. He was in college, smack in the middle of a semester, when the audition came up.

James had no idea what *Dawson's Creek* was. At first he didn't even want to tie himself to a television series. But his agent immediately saw the potential of the series. The part of Dawson Leery could easily make someone a star. It was the kind of role that could affect audiences tremendously.

James didn't think he had much of a

chance of getting the part. He thought he was too old to play a fifteen-year-old. Still, he was encouraged to give it a try.

James flew to California and read for Kevin Williamson, the casting director, and a few people from the WB network, including executive producer Paul Stupin. James submitted a résumé, was handed a script, and was asked to look it over. After flipping anxiously through the script, he was asked to turn to a certain page and read what was marked off. James read the scene and thought he'd done a pretty good job. Williamson and Stupin were immediately impressed but didn't give James an answer right away.

Instead, James waited—and wondered. He went back to Drew University and returned to the daily routine of college studies. Then the call came. James had been cast as Dawson Leery, but there was one problem. He would have to meet with Williamson and Stupin again. He did.

"Someone made a comment about my hair being too long. So Paul drove me around frantically to get me a haircut," says James.

That was it. Once his hair had been cut, both Williamson and Stupin knew they had found Dawson.

———

In the blink of an eye, James flew to the set in Wilmington, North Carolina. The pilot was filmed in May 1997.

James regards the character of Dawson as the role closest to his own personality. After playing the not-so-nice Rick in *Angus*, James was ready to prove his acting talents in a lead, nice-guy role. There are obvious similarities between James and Dawson. For one thing, James relates to the small-town life depicted in the series.

"I grew up in a small town in Connecticut so I think we show pretty universal issues," he explains. "I think people will relate to that. Also, I think there's an element of a sort of fantasy of 'I wish I grew up in a town like that.' It's just a sweet little town and I think it will be nice for people to just sort of curl up and watch and enjoy."

From the beginning, James felt that the show was daring but authentic. "The dialogue isn't necessarily representative of the way every kid speaks, but it's absolutely representative of the way every kid feels," he says. "I think that's much more important."

James has received rave reviews for his sensitive portrayal of Dawson. When he was asked during an interview to explain why he thinks *Dawson's Creek* is so popular, he said, "The show is incredibly honest. It doesn't shy away from issues. It speaks about them very frankly and honestly, without sugar-coating them. The characters on *Dawson's* make mistakes. Sometimes things blow up in their faces. But what's nice is that their mistakes are never motivated by malice, just a lack of experience."

Of course, another reason why *Dawson's Creek* has become such a hit with viewers is James himself. As one magazine has pointed out, "James is one of the best-looking babes to hit prime time in a long time."

Although he blushes when he hears things like that, James is extremely flattered to be receiving fan mail. "I try to read every letter," he confides. "And I try to answer every one. I really am grateful for every letter I get." With the mail for James continuing to pour into the offices at the WB network, it's getting harder for him to keep up with it.

Many of James's fans want to know what he's like offscreen. Could he really be as sweet and sensitive as Dawson? His answer is yes. "Dawson is a tragically nice guy, and so am I," says the star.

James feels very fortunate to have had the opportunities he's been given. He says the feeling he gets from acting is "a feeling beyond comparison. It's so exciting!"

Although he plans to stay on *Dawson's Creek* as long as it's on the air, he would also like to do more movies. He recently appeared in the film *I Love You . . . I Love You Not* with Claire Danes, and is in the independent feature film *Harvest.* "I know I'll be an actor all my life," says James with assurance. His goals are endless, and he's determined to attain every one!

James in Private

When he has some time away from the set, James likes to go home and visit his family. Besides his passion for playing all kinds of sports, James also enjoys writing. He's always scribbling down ideas for stories and poems.

James's poetry has become a big part of his life. He writes about what he sees around him, things that inspire him every day.

James likes to write so much that he has seriously thought about going into writing professionally. "If I ever get the time, I plan on writing either a screenplay or a novel," he says. "I have so many ideas. I just want to get them down on paper."

When James isn't exercising his thoughts by writing, he's exercising his body at the gym. His favorite day of the week is Saturday, because that's when he can catch up on all the things he has no time for on weekdays. He usually heads to the gym for a workout session.

The young superstar cares about his appearance and is dedicated to keeping in shape and staying healthy. His mom, Melinda, runs a gymnastics studio, and she instilled the importance of exercising in her children from a young age. Fortunately, James is blessed with natural good looks and is certainly as handsome offscreen as he is on.

James remains modest and down-to-earth about his skyrocketing success. Despite his sudden fame and fortune, he hasn't gone Hollywood. He prefers to stay home and listen to music. That helps him unwind from the everyday pressures of show business.

James always has music playing at home. He likes all kinds of music—from rock to classical to jazz. And, of course, soundtracks from musicals like *Grease, The Fantasticks,* and *Shenandoah* are high on his list.

When James has time off, he heads for the beach. He loves water activities like swimming and waterskiing.

As far as clothes, James says he doesn't

really think about them. He doesn't like to wear anything trendy or flashy and dresses more for comfort than for fashion, usually in a T-shirt and jeans.

James can be very spontaneous. He declares, "I definitely like to do things on the spur of the moment." He admits that he is sometimes serious, but not as serious as he's perceived to be.

"Of course, I take my work seriously," he explains. "But the business should be fun. And for me, it is fun."

When James is asked if he'd like to change anything in his life, he says with confidence, "No, I wouldn't want to mess with the past at all because things might not have worked out as great as they have!"

Michelle Williams

Michelle Williams plays the role of the mysterious new girl in town, Jennifer Lindley. She is the self-described baby of the *Dawson's Creek* set, born on September 9, 1980, in rural Kalispell, Montana. Her father, Larry, is a commodities trader, and her mother, Carla, is a homemaker.

"I grew up in Montana," says Michelle. "It was wide open, beautiful, and *cold*. One winter, the temperature was lower than thirty below zero every day for over one month."

Michelle also remembers Kalispell as "a real hokey town. I mean, the town threw a party when we got our first stoplight!"

The constant cold weather persuaded

Michelle's parents to move to San Diego when she was just nine years old. The move was somewhat traumatic for Michelle; she felt out of place in her new surroundings. Like her TV character, Jen, she had to get used to being the new kid in town.

Michelle remembers, "I felt so different from all the other kids." It's a feeling she uses today to portray her character on *Dawson's Creek*. "Jen is definitely from a different world than the kids at her new school," says Michelle. "She's a New York girl who's been transplanted to a small, quiet New England town."

As a young girl Michelle had many ambitions and dreams. Always athletic, the petite actress enjoyed, of all things, boxing. "I wanted to be the heavyweight champion of the world," she says, giggling. "None of that chick-fighting featherweight stuff. I wanted to take on Tyson."

Her next and most important ambition was to become an actress. She was officially bitten by the acting bug the day her parents took her to see a play. "I was completely mesmerized," she says. "I told them I wanted to perform onstage like that. I really felt I could do it."

It wasn't long before Michelle began taking acting lessons. She also started appearing in community theater productions. She knew from the first minute she hit the stage that acting was for her. "It felt so right and so natural," she says. "I knew I had to be an actress."

Soon Michelle's dad was driving her to auditions in Los Angeles, where she immediately caught the attention of casting directors. The young blonde had exactly the look they were searching for. She first won parts in television commercials, then moved into guest-starring roles on the TV series *Baywatch, Step by Step,* and *Home Improvement.*

One acting job followed another. "I thought it was so easy in the beginning because every audition I went on, I got the job," says Michelle.

In a relatively short time, the amount of work Michelle got was astonishing, even to her. She played a wide variety of roles, from comedy to drama, and she felt it was a good beginning for what she was hoping would be a steady career as an actress.

She was looking forward to moving into feature films, but she hadn't told anyone about this dream yet. Then one day her agent phoned to tell her about an audition for a remake of the classic movie *Lassie*. She nabbed the role of April in the heartwarming 1994 family film.

She followed up her big-screen debut with another exciting part, in the science fiction movie *Species*. Michelle played the challenging role of Young Sil, a character who is half human, half alien.

Species was an interesting film to work on. Even though Michelle appears only in the early scenes, she was thrilled to be part of a big-budget, high-tech movie. *Species* is about scientist Xavier Fitch (Ben Kingsley), who creates a life-form that appears to be a perfectly normal female child but is really an alien.

The scientists plan to exterminate the "child" called Sil (Michelle), but their plans meet with disastrous results as she escapes and rapidly develops from ages twelve to twenty-one. (Sil is played by Natasha Henstridge in adult form.) The scientists realize they must stop their creation before it is too late.

H. R. Giger, who was the imagination behind the nightmarish title creature in *Alien*, created the monstrous version of Sil.

Species holds a very special place in Michelle's heart. Not only was it an exciting project to work on, but also she turned fourteen during the filming. "That was the coolest thing," she says. "The cast and crew had a big birthday party for me on the set."

It was at this time that Michelle decided to concentrate on acting on a full-time basis. Up until this point, she had been going to her regular school between acting jobs. This was becoming increasingly difficult, especially since school was a less than happy experience for her.

Ninth grade was especially hard for Michelle. "It was the most miserable time in my life," she says. "I was a total nerd. People really underestimate how tough high school can be for kids. There's pressure from all sides: You have to get good grades and look and act a certain way to fit in, and everyone thinks you need a boyfriend."

The fact that she was absent a lot because of her acting work added to the pressures of school. She would be away for months working on a movie or making guest appearances on TV shows. When she returned to school, she found it extremely hard to find friends.

"If there were good times, I don't remember them," she says, "I don't have a good memory of school. I had no friends and no one to talk to. I spent every lunch in the bathroom, hiding in a stall. It's weird to be back at school on the set of *Dawson's,* opening lockers and stuff. When we go on the set and have the big hallway scenes, I still get sweaty palms."

The thing Michelle hated the most about school was "the catty fights between the girls," she says. "The girls just didn't understand that there was life past clothes, make-up, and boys. Even the peer pressure from the guys was bad. I always enjoyed the work, just not the social part of it."

Michelle had a particularly bad experience with one girl at school who just couldn't stand the fact that Michelle was succeeding as an actress. "She used to torture me. She stole my clothes out of my gym locker and hid them," Michelle remembers. "My personal favorite was the time she sent me a fake note from this very cute boy in my class. It read 'Meet me by the back stairs at three.' Of course I felt like a big fool when I showed up and he wasn't there."

Finally, after her freshman year, Michelle

decided to leave school. Her father home-schooled her, and she did so well that she graduated from high school early, at age fifteen.

Today, when she goes home to visit her parents, she'll sometimes pick up her sister, Paige, at the same school. Michelle says, "When I see the girls I went to school with I still get the shakes and my stomach hurts. I revert to this eighth-grade mentality."

Of course, now Michelle is a popular actress on a smash-hit TV series. When she does see those girls back home, they know she has already succeeded. When Michelle was asked in one magazine if revenge is sweet, she answered honestly, "The most rewarding thing for me is not so much to throw it in their faces, but the fact that everything that is happening right now is something I've always wanted."

Michelle may be exactly where she wants to be right now with her career. But at age fifteen, the future seemed uncertain. She continued auditioning and winning small roles. But commuting to Los Angeles from San Diego was becoming a strain for her and her parents.

They decided to rent an apartment for

Michelle. "My parents took turns staying with me in Los Angeles, but eventually I wound up living on my own," she explains. "I know it's crazy. My mother was scared out of her mind. It's been a source of a lot of agony for my parents."

Life away from home isn't always easy, as Michelle, who has four siblings, found out. "I love being on my own, but I miss my family, especially my sister, Paige," she says. "She's fourteen and doing all these fun things, like going to homecoming. I have to give her advice over the phone instead of seeing her every day."

To say that Michelle has grown up quickly is an understatement. She's already packed more into her seventeen years than most people do over a lifetime. Fiercely independent and extremely ambitious, Michelle kept going on auditions until she won the roles she wanted.

Her determination paid off. She won the starring role in the TV movie *A Mother's Justice*. Then she was cast in the feature film *A Thousand Acres,* which starred Jason Robards, Jessica Lange, Michelle Pfeiffer, and Jennifer Jason Leigh. The role she played, that of Pammy, was a small one, but Michelle felt it gave her the opportunity to display her acting abilities in a serious drama.

Working with Lange and Pfeiffer was a little overwhelming for Michelle, but she did her best to learn as much as she could from them.

Michelle sought the opportunity to ask both actresses as many questions as she could. In return, they spent time with her, offering advice and explaining acting to the eager-to-learn young woman.

They also taught her how to calm down before filming a scene. "It was very intimidating at first," says Michelle. "I was working with these famous actresses, and we were dealing with a heavy subject. But Michelle Pfeiffer and Jessica Lange both put me at ease. They were helpful and sweet."

Her next job was the part of a lifetime, and Michelle was glad to get it. It was the role of Jennifer in *Dawson's Creek*. Michelle will never forget her first day of work on the *Dawson's Creek* pilot. The excitement grew as the crew scurried about, getting ready for rehearsal. She felt a million emotions that day—mostly enthusiasm mixed with a bad case of nerves. She remembers that she was immediately put at ease after meeting the show's three other stars, James Van Der Beek, Katie Holmes, and Joshua Jackson.

At the time, Michelle says, no one knew the show was going to create such a sensation. "When we did the pilot, I just thought it was a good show and a job," she says. "Kevin Williamson was there and the whole *Scream* thing was starting. At first he was goofy, funny Kevin, then all of a sudden he was cover-of-*Newsweek* Kevin. I've never been involved with anything this crazy before. All the hype caught us by surprise. We were floored."

Michelle believes *Dawson's Creek* is an honest look at teenage life. "The kind of issues that we deal with aren't the kind that should be hush-hush," she says, "because the more you deal with them, the easier they become."

She feels that playing Jen is "like slipping on a second skin. I certainly have a lot to draw upon; everybody's got a past."

The thing Michelle is most concerned about is that audiences may not like her character because Dawson develops a crush on Jen and Joey becomes jealous. "I'm afraid I'm going to get hate mail," says Michelle.

"But I'm trying my damnedest to make people like me."

She needn't worry. Fans of the show adore *all* the stars. But speaking of playing favorites, Michelle was recently asked a very interesting question. Between Pacey and Dawson, who would she go for in real life?

Her answer was simple: "Pacey's the guy you fool around with. Dawson's the one you take home to Mom."

Cover Girl

At just seventeen years old, Michelle is now enjoying seeing her face on the covers of some of her favorite magazines. She admits, "It's so unreal. When I look in the mirror after they've done my hair and makeup, it doesn't look like the person I know. This isn't the reason I got into acting—but it's a perk!"

While Michelle is definitely one of the most stylish young actresses on TV, she doesn't fuss when it comes to clothes. She likes a sophisticated, feminine look, but she insists on comfort in whatever she wears.

"I love simple, tailored clothes, but I have to feel good in them," she says. "I'm most comfortable in whatever I'm wearing when I wake up. I love pajamas!"

She also loves to stay in tip-top shape. She admits that dancing is her first love because it's the perfect way to build up her legs, but she also loves running. "I try to run four to five miles a day, but it's hard after working all day. Sometimes I'm working until ten at night."

On days off, Michelle tries to work out for at least an hour. She does a variety of exercises, including stretching, bicycling, and boxing. She still loves boxing and says it's a very challenging way to tighten up her waistline and forearms.

Exercise is also an excellent way for Michelle to work off stress. "I think kids are under the wrong impression," she says. "They think being physically fit is a lot of work, but once you get into it, it's a lot of fun, and I want to help kids realize that."

Michelle is always on the go. She says that right now her life consists of eating, sleeping, and acting—and she wouldn't want it any other way. A workaholic by nature, she would much rather be extremely busy than sit at home with nothing to do. "I get bored very easily," she says with a laugh.

Because of her super-busy schedule, Michelle always has a lot on her mind.

When she isn't studying the *Dawson's Creek* scripts, she's lining up auditions for films. She never sits still.

It was while she was on her way to an audition that Michelle ended up with a new pet. She got into her car and started to drive to the audition. She's the first to admit that she's a terrible driver: "I'm hell on wheels. When I'm on the road, stay out of the way."

Michelle says that on the way to the audition she accidentally "backed over this bird. Its wings were stuck to the ground, and it was barely alive. So I thought, 'Either I'm going to leave this bird here and feel awful or take it to the vet and be late for my audition.' Well, I put it in my car and found a vet—and now I've got this bird, since it will never fly again!"

Michelle is serious about acting and needs to concentrate fully before shooting a scene. She tries to avoid distractions on the set of *Dawson's Creek* and focuses on her lines. If she's waiting to do a scene and someone walks up with a story about her in a magazine, she finds it difficult to stay sharp.

"You can't let that part of it creep into your work," she says. "Because all the other stuff, the parties and the stories, while it's fun, is not the most important part. Everyone who really plugs away in this business does it because they really want to act."

Michelle has a positive outlook on life, and it comes from the fact that she couldn't be happier with the way things are going right now. Expressing her feelings during a recent interview, she flashed her winning smile and said, "I love my life. There's nothing about it that I want to change!"

Joshua Jackson

Joshua Jackson plays the role of Pacey Witter, Dawson's smart-aleck buddy. Joshua has spent half his life as a professional actor. An early role in a tourism commercial convinced the young go-getter to make acting his career.

Joshua has emerged as a new kind of television hero: a jokester who is both charming and cool. He seems so natural playing Pacey Witter on *Dawson's Creek* that most people think Joshua is playing himself. To a certain extent, he is.

"Pacey exists to bring a little levity into Dawson's melodramatic life," says Joshua. "He's the kind of guy who deals with everything by turning it into a joke."

Like his oddly named character, Joshua

is the practical joker of the *Dawson's Creek* set. The truth is, Joshua is always looking to have a good time. While acting is serious business to him, he likes to break the tension with his cast-mates by cracking them up.

Michelle says, "Josh is the funniest guy alive. He's always finding a way to make us laugh."

Joshua entered the world on June 11, 1978, in Vancouver, British Columbia. He spent the first eight years of his life in California. He first realized his love for performing when he joined the San Francisco Boys' Chorus.

His family returned to Vancouver when his mom got a job as the casting director for the TV series *MacGyver,* which was shot in Vancouver.

Young Joshua would visit his mom at work, and started to become interested in acting. At age nine, he begged his mom to send him on auditions. She hesitated at first but finally gave in. If Joshua wanted to act, she wasn't going to stand in his way.

"I just always thought acting looked like a lot of fun," says Joshua. "And as a little kid, I wanted to do it. I don't even know why. I just wanted to see my face on the screen."

Soon he got his wish. After just a few auditions, he was cast in a series of commercials that aired in the United States promoting tourism in British Columbia.

From the first moment Joshua appeared onscreen, he captured attention. He didn't have to work hard at being appealing. He just stepped in front of the camera and flashed his million-dollar smile and people were won over. He followed up his commercials with a guest-starring role on *MacGyver*.

While Joshua always expected to make it big as an actor, he didn't suppose it would happen instantly. Even though he was certainly off to a good start, he didn't take the world by storm with his early acting stints. There was a lot to learn, and he'd have to take small roles and slowly build an impressive list of credits. But Joshua was willing to pay his dues. He was in no rush to become a flash-in-the-pan young star who burns too quickly, then fades away.

The questions Joshua asked himself at the young age of nine were "How much time do I need? How many years should I work before getting the role I want?" Joshua always had the figure of ten years in the back of his mind. But if it had taken twenty, he'd have still done it. He knew acting was what he wanted to do.

Like most actors getting started, Joshua gained early experience in regional theater. The performance that stands out in his mind was the lead role of Charlie Bucket in a Seattle-based musical production of *Willy Wonka and the Chocolate Factory.* Joshua had a ball singing songs like "I've Got a Golden Ticket." When he played the part, the movie was high on his favorite list, and he still enjoys it today.

He made his big-screen debut in Michael Bortman's critically acclaimed 1991 film *Crooked Hearts.* With an ensemble cast that included Vincent D'Onofrio, Jennifer Jason Leigh, Peter Berg, Juliette Lewis, and Marg Helgenberger, *Crooked Hearts* tells the story of a family's struggle to give each other room to grow.

Joshua was amazed to find himself on the set of a movie. Even though he had a tiny part, he says, "I had the best time on that set. I learned so much about making movies and about acting."

He followed up *Crooked Hearts* with *The Mighty Ducks,* which would become one of the most important films in his life. He would have the opportunity to reprise his role as Charlie Conroy in the film's two sequels.

The Mighty Ducks starred Emilio Estevez as Gordon Bombay, a lawyer who is assigned 500 hours of community service after being convicted of a drunk-driving charge. As part of his community service, he finds himself coaching a hockey team of misfit kids. At the time of its release in October 1992, Emilio Estevez said, "This film has a lot of heart and a lot of humor."

Emilio received most of the acclaim when the film opened to great notices. But audiences also wanted to know more about the kids who played the Mighty Ducks. Joshua wasn't lost in the shuffle. He received good reviews and stood out from the group. He gave a solid, creditable performance in a movie that scored big at the box office.

This early success might have been part of a happy time for Joshua, but in the midst of his excitement he had to face trouble at home. His parents divorced. They had been married ten years, and Joshua says, "My mother and father breaking up was tough. It was really painful because everything you

James Van Der Beek

plays the role of Dawson Leery, a hopeless romantic who wants to be the next Steven Spielberg.

James in his first film appearance, the 1995 film *Angus,* in which he played an arrogant jock.

James and costar Ariana Richards in *Angus*.

The sweet
smile of
television's
newest
heartthrob.

(Copyright © 1998
by Walter McBride/
Retna Ltd.)

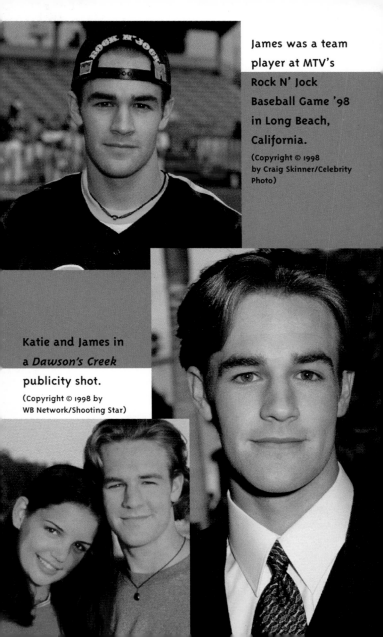

James was a team player at MTV's Rock N' Jock Baseball Game '98 in Long Beach, California.

(Copyright © 1998 by Craig Skinner/Celebrity Photo)

Katie and James in a *Dawson's Creek* publicity shot.

(Copyright © 1998 by WB Network/Shooting Star)

James and *Dawson's Creek* cast-mates Joshua Jackson, Katie Holmes, and Michelle Williams.

(Copyright © 1998 by WB Network/Shooting Star)

James looks handsome in jacket and tie.

(Copyright © 1997 by Gilbert Flores/Celebrity Photo)

At the 1998 NATPE convention in New Orleans, Michelle and James have fun.

(Copyright © 1998 by Walter McBride/Retna Ltd.)

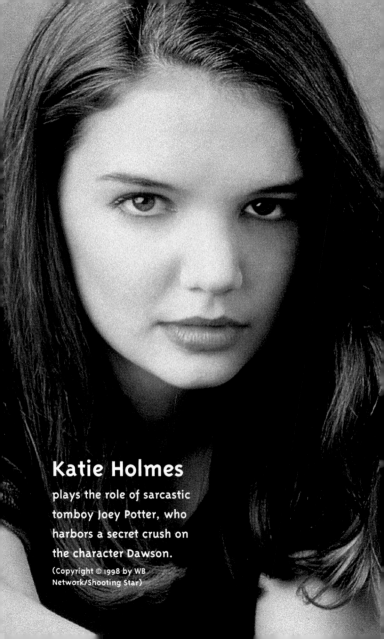

Katie Holmes

plays the role of sarcastic
tomboy Joey Potter, who
harbors a secret crush on
the character Dawson.

A well-dressed pair: James and Katie out on the town doing publicity for *Dawson's Creek*.

(Copyright © 1997 by Gilbert Flores/Celebrity Photo)

Good news for Katie! She will soon star in the thriller *Disturbing Behavior*.

(Copyright © 1997 by Miranda Shen/Celebrity Photo)

Katie's from Toledo, Ohio—like her TV character, Joey, she's a small-town girl.

(Copyright © 1997 by Gilbert Flores/Celebrity Photo)

On- and offscreen, Katie and her cast-mates are friends.

(Copyright © 1997 by Miranda Shen/Celebrity Photo)

Katie looking pretty and pensive.

(Copyright © 1997 by Kevin Winter/Celebrity Photo)

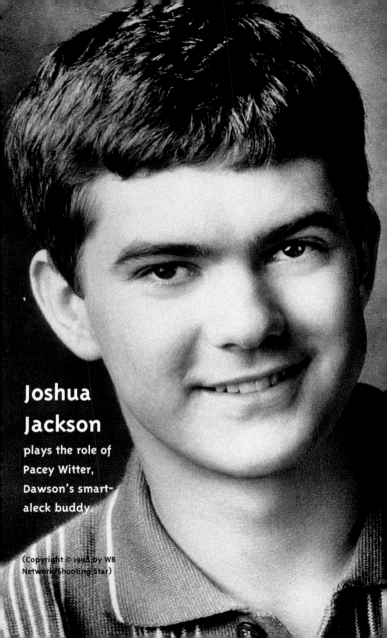

**Joshua
Jackson**

plays the role of
Pacey Witter,
Dawson's smart-
aleck buddy.

(Copyright © 1998 by WB
Network/Shooting Star)

Joshua was featured in the 1995 film *Magic in the Water*. Here he is with costars Sarah Wayne and Mark Harmon.

(Copyright © 1995 by Columbia/Tri-Star/Shooting Star)

Joshua with Willie Nark-Orn and Sarah Wayne in *Magic in the Water*. Joshua's film credits also include all three *Mighty Ducks* films, *Andre,* and *Tombstone*.

(Copyright © 1995 by Columbia/Tri-Star/Shooting Star)

Joshua
hails from
Vancouver,
Canada.

Joshua and James
Van Der Beek are
real-life
roommates.
Here's Joshua
with his roomie
and Michelle
Williams.

(Copyright © 1998 by
Walter McBride/Retna
Ltd.)

Looking sharp!
(Copyright © 1998 by Joseph
Marzullo/Retna Ltd.)

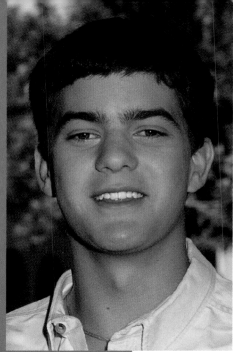

Joshua, like his character, Pacey, enjoys joking around with his *Dawson's Creek* costars!

(Copyright © 1997 by Gilbert Flores/Celebrity Photo)

Joshua joshing around with his cast-mates.
(Copyright © 1997 by Miranda Shen/Celebrity Photo)

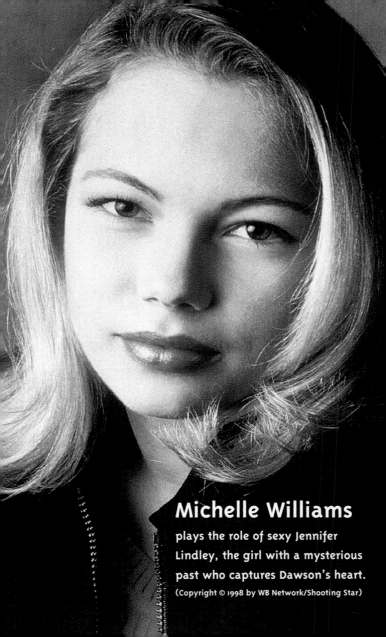

Michelle Williams

plays the role of sexy Jennifer
Lindley, the girl with a mysterious
past who captures Dawson's heart.

(Copyright © 1998 by WB Network/Shooting Star)

Michelle in the 1994 film *Lassie*.

(Copyright © 1994 by Paramount/Shooting Star)

In the 1995 film *Species,* Michelle was the young Sil, the alien portrayed as a full-grown life-form by Natasha Henstridge.

(Copyright © 1995 by Metro Goldwyn Mayer/Shooting Star)

Michelle at MTV's Rock N' Jock Baseball Game '98.

(Copyright © 1998 by Craig Skinner/ Celebrity Photo)

Michelle and Scott Foley at a _Teen People Magazine_ party.

The _Dawson's Creek_ cast at work.

trusted and felt secure about fell apart. After their divorce, I felt anything could happen."

Joshua continued to have good relations with both of his parents, but there was no denying the fact that the bottom had fallen out of his world. His way of letting off steam was first to act and second to excel at sports of every kind—baseball, football, basketball, and hockey. Joshua used sports as a way of making friends and becoming popular in school. He was also the class clown.

At this time, Joshua spent half his year on major movie and television sets and the other half in school. This posed a bit of a problem. By the time he entered high school, he craved attention and would do anything to get it.

"I used to get into so much trouble," he says. "Cracking jokes and talking when I wasn't supposed to. I would get teachers so mad, they would tell me, 'Just get out of the class.' "

Despite his reputation as a troublemaker and the fact that he was frequently absent, Joshua did well in his studies. However, although Joshua describes himself as "just an average kid in high school," he was kicked out twice. "At fifteen, I didn't take things seriously," he says. "And I got kicked out of high school twice—once for attitude and once for lack of attendance. I'd like to say that it was because I was working a lot. But really, I was just a pain in the butt." He earned his General Educational Development diploma in 1997.

From 1992 to 1994, Joshua played small parts in several films, including *Andre, Digger, Magic in the Water,* and *Tombstone.*

On the small screen, he starred in two Showtime Contemporary Classics. He played John Prince, Jr., in *Robin of Loxley,* an updated version of the Robin Hood legend. He also nabbed the lead role in *Ronnie and Julie,* a modern interpretation of *Romeo and Juliet.* And he guest-starred in the Showtime anthology *The Outer Limits.*

One of the brightest spots in Joshua's career was playing a recurring role on the short-lived TV series *Champs.* Joshua was hoping the show, which was created and produced by Gary David Goldberg *(Family Ties, Spin City),* would be a hit, but it turned out to be a big disappointment. It was canceled before it even had a chance to draw an audience.

In 1994 Joshua reprised his role in the successful sequel to *The Mighty Ducks,* called *D2: The Mighty Ducks.* The entire cast returned, slightly older but ready to bring back the magic of *The Mighty Ducks.*

In the second film, the plot involved Gordon Bombay (Emilio Estevez) and his team of hockey players representing America in an international hockey competition.

The popularity of *D2: The Mighty Ducks* led to *D3: The Mighty Ducks,* a third installment of this family favorite. By this time, Joshua was a senior in high school. He and his young costars had grown up on the *Mighty Ducks* films. Not only had he grown almost five inches since the first film, but he was now more serious about acting and what he wanted to do with his future.

In *D3,* the young hockey champions accept athletic scholarships from exclusive Eden Hall Academy. When Ducks coach Gordon Bombay (Emilio Estevez) does not immediately accompany them to Eden Hall, the team feels abandoned. In *D3,* the coolest team on ice has a new school and a new coach. Joshua's character is promoted to captain of the team, and the same old Ducks attitude shines through as they face off against an upper-class hockey team and school alumni who threaten to revoke the Ducks' scholarships. Although not their coach in this film, Emilio still makes an appearance as the team's lawyer.

Over the course of the three films, Emilio made a big impact on the young cast. Producer Jordan Kerner says, "Emilio symbolizes for the kids a big brother they can look up to." Joshua especially enjoyed working with him. "I grew up watching Emilio in movies like *The Outsiders, The Breakfast Club,* and *St. Elmo's Fire,*" says Joshua. "It was terrific working with him."

Emilio was equally impressed with his young costars. "They're good people, and to see how they've changed over the years is really wonderful," he said during the production of *D3.*

One thing that didn't change during the production of the three films was that the kids gave Emilio a tough time when he had to skate. "They would constantly tease me about being a terrible skater," he says. "I'm not that terrible, but I'm not that great either. Being from Southern California, skating isn't something you think about doing very often. So they thought it was very funny every time I fell on the ice."

Joshua, on the other hand, was a pro on the ice. Since he was from Canada, he had practically grown up playing hockey.

Joshua has nothing but good things to say about his *Mighty Ducks* experience. "It was a life-changing thing after the first movie came out," he says. "It's like there's a *Mighty Ducks* cult. Kids watch the movies over and over and it's great to have that kind of reaction."

Joshua says it helped that the group of young actors became friends off the set, keeping in close contact between films.

The *Mighty Ducks* movies were so successful that the Walt Disney Company acted quickly on an opportunity to buy a National Hockey League franchise. In 1996 the Mighty Ducks of Anaheim were born.

Joshua thinks it's amazing that there is an actual hockey team called the Mighty Ducks. "When the kids who watch the movie and who've grown up with the movie become adults and if everybody on earth forgets about the movies, there will always be the legacy of the Anaheim Mighty Ducks that we left behind," he says. "It's a really cool thing.

It just puts it on a whole different level. It's indescribable. It feels like being immortal."

After his success in the *Mighty Ducks* films, Joshua thought he couldn't possibly be in anything that successful again. He was wrong. His life took another amazing turn in late 1996 when he was cast in a tiny role as Film Class Guy #1 in *Scream 2*. He had hoped to get a bigger part in the film, but he wasn't complaining.

As it turned out, accepting that small role was a smart decision. One day on the set Joshua met the film's screenwriter, Kevin Williamson, who was in the middle of searching for the right actors for the lead roles in *Dawson's Creek*.

Joshua was at the right place at the right time. When he heard about the audition, he immediately went in to read for the role of Dawson. When he didn't get that part, he was offered the role of Pacey.

"It worked out great because Pacey is closer to my own personality," says Joshua. He describes Pacey as "the youngest, oddball child in an authoritative family, and the only way he can deal is to be as big a screwup as possible. Pacey just can't plug into society. He just does what he does and doesn't worry about the consequences."

Joshua is looking forward to playing Pacey for years. "I hope the show runs forever," he declares.

Next, Joshua will costar with Brad Renfro and Ian McKellen in Bryan Singer's *Apt Pupil,* based on a Stephen King story. Looking ahead, Joshua says he plans to act for a long time. "I don't know what I'd do if I didn't act," he says. "It lets my feelings show. And that's why I love it!"

Two Sides of Joshua

Joshua has a healthy attitude about his success. He's been through so much already that he can put it all into perspective.

"I'm aware that I am not going to be a star of a series forever," he says. "But I do know that I'm in this business for good."

He has talent to burn and a tremendous amount of confidence in himself. He had it when he was young and unknown, and he has it now. After ten years of appearing in a variety of roles, Joshua has achieved his dream of success. He is finally where he wants to be in his career, but he's careful not to get caught up in the trappings of Hollywood.

People who have worked with Joshua are enormously impressed by his dedication.

"I've worked on TV shows where the actors come in, hit their marks, and then ask, 'When will we wrap for lunch?' " says one member of the *Dawson's* crew. "That's not Joshua. We'll be on the set sometimes until ten P.M. Everyone is exhausted and he'll still be trying to keep us going, telling jokes. He's a great guy."

One critic said of Joshua's immense talent, "One of these days he's going to pull something out of the bottom of his soul and knock everyone out."

He seems to be doing just that in every episode of *Dawson's Creek*. If he isn't knocking everyone out with his amazing talent, he's doing it with his energy. Although the *Dawson's* production schedule can sometimes be grueling, Joshua is always ready for action.

But there's more to him than meets the eye. Joshua may be known as a cutup and a compulsive practical joker, but there's another side to this sensitive star. Joshua is the kind of guy who thoroughly appreciates everything that has happened in his life and career. He's thrilled to be working on a top-rated TV series and loves meeting his fans.

"The other day I was in a video store," he says, "and a seven-year-old kid came up to me and said, 'Hey, it's Charlie!'" (That was Joshua's character in the three *Mighty Ducks* films.) "Now, that's really nice!"

He says being recognized for his role in *Dawson's Creek* is twice as nice. When fans line up to meet him and get his autograph, he makes sure everyone goes away happy. "I love my fans and I love when they come up and ask for an autograph. It's very flattering," he says. "So if you see me in a store or anywhere, don't be shy. Come up and say hello."

Joshua also loves receiving fan mail. "Many of the letters I get are from young people," he says. "Because of my age and the bond they have with the show, I feel I have an obligation to them. I always try to project a positive influence."

Right now Joshua is dividing his time between his home in Vancouver and the set of *Dawson's Creek* in Wilmington, North Carolina. He finds it's sometimes difficult to stay close to his family and friends because he's working all the time. But maintaining a good relationship with the people back home is at the top of his priority list.

Joshua has had some of his friends from home visit him at work. "To keep a friendship going, I sometimes invite one of my friends to the set," he says. "I try to call my family a couple of times a week, and my sister just loves coming to visit. I feel it's important to stay close to family and friends. I try not to let the show get in the way. Of course, it takes up more of my time, but I don't let it take up all my time."

It's clear that Joshua is completely unspoiled by his success. He's 100 percent down-to-earth. Success couldn't have happened to a nicer guy!

Katie Holmes

"**I**'m a tomboy like Joey, but I'm a little bit more shy," says Katie Holmes, who plays Joey on *Dawson's Creek*.

Katie stepped into her role as Dawson's best friend with incredible ease. "Only a few girls get to be prom queens and get all the guys," Katie says. "Those girls are like Jen. Joey isn't the girl who gets all the guys. I wasn't like that, either, so I can relate."

The only thing she finds hard to relate to is Joey's tragic childhood. Her character has lost her mother to cancer and her father is in jail, so she lives with her sister, Bessie.

Katie's life has been much easier than Joey's. Born on December 18, 1978, Katie grew up with a loving family in Toledo, Ohio. Katie is the youngest of five; her mother is a homemaker and her father is a lawyer. As a young girl, Katie dreamed of becoming an actress. But it was a dream she put on hold until she entered high school.

In her freshman year, Katie signed up for a drama class and began acting in school productions. She loved it but remained realistic. "I really wanted to be an actress, but I'm from Ohio," she says. "I told myself, 'Get a grip.'"

She realized that the only way to make her dreams come true was to leave Ohio. Despite her love for her hometown and her family, Katie knew that if she was going to break into acting, she would have to leave home.

Katie's life was changed forever the day she heard about a modeling and talent convention being held in New York City. Katie wanted to attend, and her mother agreed to go with her.

New York was the land of promise for Katie. The vast city with its bright lights and twenty-four-hour-a-day action was an exciting symbol of freedom for a girl from small-town America. Katie knew if she could get to New York, she'd have a chance at making her dreams reality.

And she was right. She met a talent manager at the modeling convention who encouraged her to go to Los Angeles and audition for TV's pilot season.

Katie took this advice and went on her very first professional audition. To her surprise, she was cast in a small role in the acclaimed film *The Ice Storm*.

Because she was cast on the spot, Katie didn't have a chance to audition for anything else. In a remarkably short period, she was whisked to the set of *The Ice Storm* and began working. She was thrilled to be on the set with some of the biggest-name actors in the business and to be directed by a famous director.

The Ice Storm, directed by Ang Lee *(Sense and Sensibility),* won the Best Screenplay award at the 1997 Cannes Film Festival. It starred Kevin Kline, Sigourney Weaver, Joan Allen, and a host of young actors including Christina Ricci and Elijah Wood. Katie portrayed Libbets Casey, the spaced-out, rich girlfriend of Paul Hood (Tobey Maguire).

Katie approached her first role with zeal and set out to "be the best that I can be." Ang Lee encouraged the actors to contribute to their characters. The film takes place in

1973. Katie remembers that during one meeting, Christina Ricci said, referring to the film's teenage cast, "In 1973, we weren't born yet!"

The Ice Storm remains one of Katie's most treasured memories. She valued the opportunity to work with Ang Lee, one of today's most creative directors. She also appreciated the chance to meet and get to know other actors of her generation. She became friends with Christina, Elijah, and Tobey. Even though they did their share of partying, they are all serious and dedicated when it comes to acting. Katie would often talk to them about acting and the roles they had already played.

Katie's part didn't require her to be on the set long, but she felt that the time she spent working on *The Ice Storm* was incredibly valuable. The fact that her part was a relatively small one didn't seem to bother her.

Most actors would have followed up such a great beginning with a series of auditions. But after *The Ice Storm,* Katie did something shocking. She went back home to finish high school. This move surprised her agent, who was on the phone lining up more auditions for her.

Katie had other plans. She was now a senior in high school, and she didn't want to miss out on her last year. She opted to audition for school plays instead of TV shows and films. She tried out for the school production of the musical *Damn Yankees* and was cast in the lead role of Lola.

At the same time, her agent called to tell her about a new TV series called *Dawson's Creek,* for which auditions were being held. Katie's agent thought she'd be perfect for one of the roles. The producers of *Dawson's Creek* made it clear that they weren't looking for actors with big credits. They wanted fresh new faces.

Katie was scheduled to fly to L.A. to try out for *Dawson's Creek.* The only problem was getting to the audition. She was rehearsing *Damn Yankees* and didn't want to disappoint her classmates because of a role she might not get.

Katie finally reached an agreement with her agent and the producers of *Dawson's Creek.* Instead of auditioning for them in person, she sent them a videotape from her home in Toledo. The bold move may have actually worked in her favor. Her acting wowed the producers of *Dawson's Creek*. She was exactly what they were looking for.

In a very short time, she got a callback. They were interested in her for the role of Joey Potter, but they had to meet her in person. While Katie was thrilled with the news, there was one minor problem. The callback conflicted with her play's opening night. She had been rehearsing her role, which required a great deal of singing as well as acting, almost every day after school for weeks. She couldn't let all that work go to waste.

Instead of jumping at the chance to meet with the *Dawson's Creek* producers, this very independent young woman chose to decline the callback. Luckily, the producers were willing to wait. Katie rescheduled her audition, and she landed the role of Joey.

It was the big break that every actor longs for. Some actors wait years for something like this to happen, and unfortunately, most never get it at all. But for Katie it happened very quickly.

Katie was familiar with her three costars and their work. She knew they had more experience than she did, and she admits she was a little intimidated by them at first.

"They are very worldly," she explains. "But they are teaching me."

Does Katie like to watch herself on TV every week? "Yes, definitely," she says, beaming. "It's not only very exciting to see myself on TV, but I learn from it. I can figure out what I may or may not want to do in the future.

"The others will all probably say, 'Oh no, I won't watch,'" she continues. "But I'll admit that I'll be watching it, thinking, *Oh, my God! I thought they were going to use a different take.*"

Katie feels very fortunate to be part of *Dawson's Creek*. She believes the contrasts among the characters' words, feelings, and actions are what gives the show its emotional punch. "It gives it a kind of a nice tone when we're analyzing and we're using big words, but at the same time we're doing the same stupid things that everybody does," she says.

Her character is described as a sarcastic tomboy, but Katie feels that Joey's sarcasm really covers up the fact that she's attracted to Dawson. "Joey has to come back with her wit," says Katie. "It's the only way she knows how to deal with her crush on Dawson and her hard times at home."

How do her parents feel when they watch their daughter deliver some of the show's racier dialogue? "Oh, they don't mind," says Katie. "They just kind of laugh."

Katie is one of the fortunate few who has managed to blast off into an acting career almost as soon as she reached the launchpad. So far she has auditioned for three roles, landing all three: *The Ice Storm, Dawson's Creek,* and the upcoming feature film *Disturbing Behavior.*

Katie was psyched to win the lead role in *Disturbing Behavior.* James Marsden and Nick Stahl (who was in *The Man Without a Face* with Mel Gibson) are her costars. In this teen chiller, Katie plays a girl from the wrong side of the tracks. "She's the kind of girl you don't want your son to date," she says.

Disturbing Behavior is about a town that is mysteriously transforming its young people into strangely perfect citizens. Katie says of the film, "It's not far from reality and that makes it even more frightening. I just hope this doesn't happen to anyone I know."

As far as working both in movies and on

TV, Katie can't decide which she prefers. "I'm having fun doing both," she says with a smile. "I just like to work."

It almost seems as if Katie was destined to become a star. But she's modest about her success. Right now, she's trying to keep her feet on the ground and everything in perspective.

When the pressures of the business start to mount, Katie heads home to Toledo. One of the things that helps keep her on an even keel is her family. If she has a problem, she can go to them. Katie considers her mom one of her best friends. And she's equally close to her dad and siblings.

Katie is also still close friends with the kids she grew up with. After a few days of hanging out with her hometown pals, she's completely refreshed and ready to get back to work—and to the limelight!

"Everything is happening so quickly," she sighs. "Success is about getting an education and being happy. I don't think there's any mark I can make. And if I did think that, my family would knock me over the side of the head, like, 'Who do you think you are?' I'm taking each day as it comes. I'm just having fun!"

There's no denying that being on *Dawson's Creek* is a life-changing experience for Katie. Because of the show, she has put college on hold. She was to begin her freshman year at Columbia University, but she delayed her admission to star in *Dawson's Creek*.

However, college is definitely going to be part of Katie's future. "In five years, I would like to see myself either having a diploma from college or in the process of achieving it," she says. Right now, though, *Dawson's Creek* is her priority.

What has been the biggest change in Katie's life since she began working on the show? "It would have to be that I can buy nicer gifts for people," she says. "I think all of us on the show feel like that. But it's not like we are going overboard and shopping all the time. I think we have good heads on our shoulders."

Katie's Style

Katie hasn't let her sudden burst of fame go to her head. She is as level-headed as she was before *Dawson's Creek* came along.

Katie describes herself as very energetic, determined, and emotional. Her weakness, she says, is being overly sensitive. When people praise her work, she can't help responding in an emotional way. "Sometimes I am so happy that I start to cry," she says.

Katie is being looked up to as a role model and trendsetter. She's already graced the covers of *Seventeen* and *Teen* and is a natural model. She admits that her style has always been unconventional.

"Basically I like to wear what I feel comfortable in," she says. "I love short skirts, but I also like pants with a short, cropped top."

Katie prefers the natural look in makeup. The only time she wears heavy makeup is for photo sessions and under the hot lights of the *Dawson's Creek* cameras.

Katie's beauty program extends to her diet. Despite her cravings for junk food, she's a wise eater. "You can eat anything you want as long as you eat a little of it," she advises. "Eating in moderation is the key to staying slim."

Generally, Katie eats the kinds of foods that nutritionists recommend for staying healthy—chicken, fresh vegetables, and salads.

She doesn't smoke, and she exercises daily.

Katie doesn't really have to worry about keeping her weight down, but she is careful to get enough protein. Before she starts her day, she mixes a breakfast drink with powdered protein in it. She believes this gives her an extra boost of energy. Katie also believes in taking vitamins. If she thinks she isn't getting enough from her diet, she takes supplements.

Despite the dizzying success of *Dawson's Creek,* Katie has been handling it all pretty well. She does admit that it took a little getting used to. "When they sent me on photo shoots and interviews, I wasn't ready for them," she says.

Katie is concerned with looking her absolute best at all times. One day while a photographer from a magazine was visiting the *Dawson's Creek* set, Katie covered her face with her script. Katie was supposed to look exhausted in one scene, and the makeup person had drawn dark bags under her eyes. The photographer tried to get a photo of her, but she kept her face covered and wouldn't allow him to snap her.

"I looked awful," she says. "I didn't want those photos circulating and possibly landing at the *National Enquirer.* After all, I had makeup on for a scene."

The real Katie is strong-minded and ambitious. But she is also extremely honest. She's modest about her success and very friendly.

Katie and her costars are high on the list of young stars making a big impact. Of course, Katie enjoys hearing this news, even if she finds it hard to believe. Only a few years ago she was just a regular teenager, going to school and hanging out with her friends. "I haven't had a chance to think all this through yet," she says. "But it's great to be an inspiration to someone else!"

On the Set

Dawson's Creek is shot three thousand miles away from Hollywood, in Wilmington, North Carolina. It's cheaper to shoot in North Carolina than it is in California. Besides, Wilmington seems the perfect stand-in for *Dawson's Creek*'s fictional Capeside, Massachusetts. There are sets for everything: Dawson's house, the S.S. Icehouse where Joey waitresses, and the Screen Play video store where Dawson and Pacey work. An old *Matlock* set is used for scenes inside Capeside High School.

The first film to be shot in Wilmington was the 1984 horror movie *Firestarter,* which starred Drew Barrymore. Since that time, Wilmington has been the setting for many movies and TV shows. Kevin Williamson's

I Know What You Did Last Summer was filmed in Wilmington, as well as TV series like *Matlock* and the short-lived *American Gothic*.

For the most part, the actors are happy to be working far from Hollywood. Being so far away, they don't have to deal with the full stress of their newfound fame. James says, "It's extremely overwhelming, but it's not part of our daily reality down in Wilmington."

Of course, the local fans do ask for autographs or to have their pictures taken with the young stars. A photo of the cast was hung on the wall of a local coffee shop where the cast-mates hang out. But other than that, James, Joshua, Katie, and Michelle live pretty normal lives in Wilmington.

A typical day on the *Dawson's Creek* set begins early in the morning. It isn't uncommon for the group to work twelve- or sixteen-hour days.

Before any shooting begins, the cast goes through a cold reading of the script. Next, as the cameras are positioned, the actors report to Hair and Makeup. In the theater, actors do their own makeup, but in films and TV these jobs are done by professionals who know what will look right under certain lights and from various camera angles.

Next comes Wardrobe, where clothes are provided for each actor. When the show first began, the producers had a very specific idea of what the actors should wear. Now, as each actor grows into his or her role, each can suggest what might look right. The company that provides the clothes for *Dawson's Creek* is J. Crew.

The *Dawson's Creek* set is an extremely pleasant one with a real hometown atmosphere. Most of the crew members live in Wilmington.

Because everyone in the cast is so young and so enthusiastic about being part of such a great show, the *Dawson's Creek* set seems very comfortable. The actors try to be considerate of each other.

For example, when James and Michelle have a scene together, Katie usually leaves the set so that they can turn in the best possible performance. "A lot of times I don't want to intrude on the others," she says. "It's uncomfortable enough to get yourself up in front of the camera."

When the cameras stop rolling for the day, the foursome rarely splits up. They get along so well, they hang out in downtown Wilmington on their days off.

"We go to same restaurant every night, and we order the same things," says Michelle. "Oh, God, they have the best restaurants here in Wilmington. We all have big appetites."

Their favorite restaurant is called the Deluxe. It's right downstairs from the apartment James and Joshua share.

While shooting the first season of shows, the actors shared an apartment with Joshua's black Labrador-Rhodesian Ridgeback mix, Shumba. "It's worked out," says James. "Fortunately, we've managed not to kill each other. We get along very well." He pauses, then adds with a laugh, "But Josh is sometimes bizarre."

Joshua is definitely the comedian of the foursome. He loves to crack up the gang even when they're in the middle of shooting a scene.

"When I have to cry for the camera, I can always count on Josh being off to the side mooning me," says Michelle. "I've seen that boy's butt more times than I care to say."

Because Joshua is always playing jokes on his costars, they decided to give him a dose of his own medicine. Everyone, including the director and the entire crew, were in on one joke they played on Joshua.

"We were in a field, finishing the last shot of the day," Joshua remembers. "I said my line and turned to walk away, but no one yelled, 'Cut.' So I kept walking until I finally turned around and realized that everyone had left without me."

Then there are the little mistakes that give everyone a good laugh. Michelle recalls one such incident. "We were doing a scene where we had to slide down the halls," she says. "We did a test run, and everything was okay—but I'm not the most coordinated person. The cameras rolled, I tripped over my own feet and went flying across the hall. They played it back and forth on the monitor in slow motion, then in fast motion, and it entertained everyone for an hour."

These kinds of high jinks make the *Dawson's Creek* set a happy place to work. And that relaxed atmosphere sometimes comes in handy. When it rained nonstop for an entire day, cast and crew were told that shooting would continue into the night. When they finally wrapped at three A.M., everyone was exhausted. Only Joshua had enough energy to keep everyone else's spirits up.

The fun and games started the day the fab foursome met. Back in May 1997, when they were shooting the very first episode of *Dawson's Creek,* Katie and Michelle pulled a prank on James and Joshua. They were all staying at the Howard Johnson's in Wilmington. Katie and Michelle got the bright idea to lock the guys out of their room—leaving them in the hallway in their underwear. Michelle remembers, "We just terrorized them. They didn't want to go into the lobby because they were only in their underwear."

The four actors have grown accustomed to living in Wilmington during the months they work on the show. "I love it, but I do miss being able to grocery shop at three in the morning," says Michelle.

According to James, "Wilmington is actually a great town. We hang out, go out with the crew, go out with the cast, go to the beach."

James feels that being away from Hollywood is the main reason they've all been able to deal with the pressures of filming a successful weekly show. "I'm so glad I'm not in L.A. right now. It would kill me," he says. "Doing a series is so much of a head trip as it is."

For Katie too, living and working on the show in Wilmington is an advantage. "You can't do auditions on the weekends here," she says. "And it forces the cast to bond because we don't know anyone else."

While the guys chose to share an apartment, Katie and Michelle live in their own apartments. "I'm not the easiest person to live with," admits Katie. "I'm kind of a slob. So for me to consider a roommate, it would have to be one of my sisters or something."

Katie and Michelle have become close friends. They like watching classic 1980s teen movies like *Sixteen Candles* and *Pretty in Pink* in their off time. "Katie and I make a point of finding time to goof off and be kids," says Michelle. "We bake cookies and drink a lot of coffee. I'm pretty happy to have a buddy to do girl stuff with."

The offscreen friendships among the four young stars have certainly spilled over nicely onscreen. Maybe that's the secret of their success!

The Creek in Depth

You just can't talk about *Dawson's Creek* without mentioning what happens in the show's first episodes. Whatever the future brings, these are the shows that introduced us to Dawson and his world. These are the episodes that hooked an audience of loyal fans and kept them tuning in every week to see the lives of Dawson, Joey, Pacey, and Jennifer unfolding.

Viewers were introduced to these characters in the show's first episode, "Emotions in Motion." Drawing on an arsenal of pop culture references, the involving drama opened with Dawson realizing that his lifelong friendship with his best friend, Josephine "Joey" Potter, is changing. While they're learning to deal with this, Dawson begins a romance with a new girl in town, the radiant Jennifer Lindley, who moves in with her grandmother. Jen appears to be the girl next door, but her past is a mystery. Meanwhile, Dawson's best pal, Pacey, who works with him in the local video store, is contemplating an affair with a new teacher at school, Tamara Jacobs (Leann Hunley).

The first episode was written by Kevin Williamson and directed by Steve Miner. Williamson based much of the first episode on real-life experiences. The *Chicago Sun-Times* said in its review of the show, "Williamson turns pivotal moments from his past into eloquent, carefully constructed sentences."

Most critics who reviewed the series had nothing but praise for it. *The Seattle Times* said, "*Dawson's Creek* is the best show of the 1997–98 season. It may prove to be the best coming-of-age series ever done on television."

The *San Francisco Examiner* declared, "The best new show of the season is *Dawson's Creek*. Not just the midseason. All season."

The *St. Louis Post-Dispatch* raved, "Fans of shows like *Party of Five* and *My So-Called Life* —and good TV in general—should certainly sample *Dawson's Creek*. The young actors cast as the central foursome seem destined for stardom."

No other series on TV has as many pop culture references as *Dawson's Creek*. In the premiere episode, there were forty-six, with sixteen just about Dawson's idol Steven Spielberg and his movies. "This is the way I write," confesses Williamson. "But it's not for the sake of making a reference. I try to make sure it drives the story forward." To prove he leaves nothing out, Williamson parodied his own movie *Scream* in one episode. *Scream* and *Scream 2* were themselves homages to horror movies.

Dawson's Creek gives almost as much time to its adult characters as it does to the teen characters. Dawson's parents, played by John Wesley Shipp and Mary-Margaret Humes, are trying desperately to save their troubled marriage. Jen's strict, religious grandmother (Mary Beth Peil) is concerned about her granddaughter.

On the subject of Jen's grandmother, Williamson says, "I wanted her to live and breathe and be a real human being. There's a wonderful dynamic where Jen says, 'Grams, open your mind,' and Jen ultimately realizes it's *her* mind that's not opening."

In the show's second episode, "Dirty Dancing," Dawson continues to work on his movie. He's disappointed when he discovers that Jen is going to a school dance with Cliff, their high school's football star. Dawson makes a scene at the dance that causes Jen to walk out. Later he apologizes and tells Jen how he really feels about her. She tells him she feels the same way but that she wants to move more slowly than she has in the past. Dawson understands, and they end up sharing a dance.

Because Williamson is working on many other projects, he can't write every episode of *Dawson's*. He does, however, supervise the series and says he has written three seasons' worth of outlines. "I am never that far away, and I never will be," he says. "I will always be near this show." Two women and three men in their twenties and thirties were hired as *Dawson's* writing staff, and Williamson feels confident with his show in their hands.

Writer Rob Thomas—well known for his young adult novel *Rats Saw God*— wrote the screenplay for the episode "A Prelude to a Kiss." In it, Dawson's dream of a perfect first kiss with Jen is about to come true when Jen discovers a secret that destroys their romantic moment. Meanwhile, Dawson is working on his film class's movie as a silent observer and is having a hard time keeping quiet when he sees that the film is in trouble. And at the same time, Joey finds herself swept away by a handsome stranger whose family's sailboat is docked in Capeside, and Pacey and his teacher, Tamara Jacobs, learn that their secret affair may no longer be secret.

"Carnal Knowledge" is a stirring episode that begins with the twentieth wedding anniversary of Dawson's parents. On that day, Dawson sees his mother with another man. He tells Joey, then feels betrayed when she says she has known about his mother's dishonesty all along. Jen reveals her dark past in New York to Dawson and feels him slipping away. Meanwhile, Dawson captures the romance between Pacey and Tamara Jacobs on videotape.

Williamson remarks that Dawson could well have been written as a girl because of his emotions, and Jen, who becomes his love, could have been a guy with a dark past. The switch was made purposely. "I think it's just fun to watch some of the tables get turned on some of the double standards," Williamson says.

In the episode "Blown Away," written by Williamson and Dana Baratta, the Leerys, the Potters, and Jen and her grandmother are confined to the Leery house during a hurricane. Tempers run high when Dawson and his dad confront his mother about her affair. Across town, Pacey ruins his big brother's chances with Tamara Jacobs at her beach house. Dylan Neal guest-stars as Pacey's brother, Deputy Doug Witter.

In the episode "Look Who's Talking," Joey's sister, Bessie (Nina Repeta), goes into labor at the Leery household. When Joey remembers the pain of her mother's death, she turns to Dawson for comfort. Meanwhile, rumors of Pacey's affair with Tamara Jacobs begin to spread, and the school board calls an emergency meeting to decide her fate.

The episode titled "The Breakfast Club" borrows its theme from the 1985 movie of the same name. In the original film, brat-packers Molly Ringwald, Ally Sheedy, Judd Nelson, Emilio Estevez, and Anthony Michael Hall are forced to spend a weekend in detention together. The *Dawson's Creek* episode has the gang stuck in a Saturday detention, where Dawson and Pacey turn against each other and Joey offers a tearful explanation for her anger toward Jen.

It's obvious that *Dawson's Creek* owes much to the movies. Many of its plots have been inspired by films. "From the get-go, I *was* media," says Williamson, who admits to being a pop culture junkie. "As a kid, I always went to the movies even though my dad had to drive twenty-five miles to the nearest theater." Williamson also spent much of his youth in front of the television set, and sees *Dawson's Creek* as a mix of 1970s shows *Apple's Way* and *James at 15*.

In the episode "Escape from New York," Dawson is upset when Jen's ex-boyfriend from the city (guest star Eion Bailey) shows up in Capeside to try to win her back. Meanwhile, Joey goes to a beach party with Pacey and gets drunk. The episode ends on a tantalizing note when Joey and Dawson share an unexpected kiss.

Williamson says that like the characters on *Dawson's Creek,* he was always trying to fit in. "I always tried to talk bigger than I was and smarter than I was," says Williamson. "I went from crowd to crowd. I hung out with the smokers. I hung out with the in crowd. I hung out with A students. I am really glad I did because now I have such a huge filing cabinet of information."

One reason for the show's tremendous success is that each show is designed not as a TV episode but as a one-hour movie. In fact, to give the show a cinematic look, zoom lenses are never used, as they are on regular TV shows. Instead of zooming in and out of scenes, the camera is moved on a dolly track. This extra effort gives the series a very specific look.

The Los Angeles Daily News pointed out in its review of *Dawson's Creek,* "Everything about this show—from the cast to the setting to the camera work—looks great!"

Kevin Williamson and his four stars are ecstatic over the success of the show. To get the show started, WB originally ordered thirteen episodes, which, the network believed, would take it into the summer of 1998. By March the WB announced that twenty-two additional episodes had been ordered for the second season.

While some have complained about the show's racy dialogue, others have applauded it. WB executives say they have received few complaints about the language.

James is quick to defend the show. "People were going on about all the sex in the show," he says. "What do you mean? How many people had sex in the pilot? But do fifteen-year-olds talk about sex? I mean, are they thinking about it? Yeah. We are not giving these kids any ideas, but what we do is talk about these issues. I think we do it really responsibly."

Love and Romance

*L*ove and dating are two very hot topics on *Dawson's Creek*. When the characters aren't flirting, falling in love, breaking up, or dealing with major crushes, they're talking endlessly about it.

Working on a show like *Dawson's Creek* is challenging to the actors who play the central characters. They find themselves working together closely every day. Sometimes their scenes involve passionate kissing.

For example, in the episode "The Breakfast Club," in which the stars spend Saturday in detention, they play a game of Truth or Dare. In the end, Pacey kisses Dawson's on-screen love, Jen, while Dawson shares a kiss with Joey.

Naturally, because the cast is young, gorgeous, and single, there have been rumors that their onscreen relationships are spilling over into their real lives.

Is this true? Does the onscreen friendship between James and Katie end when the cameras stop rolling? Are James and Michelle a *real* twosome?

It's a well-known fact that James, Michelle, Joshua, and Katie are close friends off the set. But that's all they are. They've never thought of dating each other. Katie says with a laugh, "I make it a point never to date an actor."

While that may be true, they also know how uncomfortable it would be if two members of the cast dated and then broke up. Right now, they're all the best of friends, and that's exactly how they want it to stay.

If the rumors continue to circulate, it's probably because of the foursome's explosive onscreen chemistry. But they attribute that to their spending a lot of time together on and offscreen. "We already know a lot about each other," says Michelle. "What we like, what we don't like. We've talked about everything."

And that includes everyone's love life. Even though they have definite ideas of the kind of person they're looking for, none of them has the time right now to think about dating. "Lately, all we've been doing is working on the show and doing a barrage of press," says Michelle.

In interviews, the four stars don't mind talking about their real-life love lives. The subject of romance is definitely on their minds, and they're willing to answer any questions they're asked.

James Van Der Beek

"I'm looking forward to meeting a girl, getting married, and starting a family," says James.

He is affectionately known as the serious romantic of the group, and he lives up to that reputation. Once he and his girlfriend had a nighttime picnic on a rooftop. Says James, "We just sat there and watched the stars."

Because of his hectic life, James doesn't have a steady girlfriend. "I haven't dated that many girls because I've been so busy," he says. "But every time I took a girl home to meet my family, it was very special to me."

Despite the fact that James has won the hearts of millions of girls everywhere, he says, "I'm still nervous and shy when I meet girls. The only thing that has changed is that

I get to meet more girls now because they introduce themselves to me."

The truth is, James finds it hard to maintain a meaningful relationship because he doesn't stay in one place long enough. He does know the kind of girl he's looking for. "I like someone who is honest and can carry on a good conversation," he says. "I'd like to get together with a girl who likes going out to a movie or concert as much as staying home and talking. To me, that's all just as important."

James doesn't like a girl who wears an overabundance of makeup. "How she acts is probably more important to me," he says. "I like a natural look, but it wouldn't matter if she was blonde, brunette, or redhead. Personality means a lot. I especially like a girl with a pretty smile."

Whoever catches this cutie will be very lucky!

Michelle Williams

"It's been a while since I've been on a date," announces Michelle. "I barely have enough time to sleep. It's been so crazy."

Although Michelle has been out on dates, she admits she isn't ready for a serious romance. While most girls her age are getting ready to go to the prom, Michelle has been busy carving out a successful acting career.

"I've never been to a prom. I was never asked," she admits. "The first time I watched *Pretty in Pink,* I thought the prom was the most magical experience I could ever have. I recently saw the movie again, and it seemed more real to me the second time."

Michelle would like to go to a prom with her girlfriends. "What could be better than looking great and being surrounded by your best friends?" she says. "But going with a special guy would be fun too. I'd probably want to leave early so we could have quiet time together."

Michelle, who lives alone, looks forward to having a guy share her life. "I just don't know how I would fit a boyfriend into my life right now," she says honestly. "It would be nice if I wasn't alone all the time, but it's giving me a chance to figure out who I am without having a guy influence my self-image."

At only seventeen, Michelle has years to search for Mr. Right.

Joshua Jackson

When Joshua is asked to describe his best dates, he flashes a devilish grin and jokes, "A good date for me is one where no one cries and no blood's been shed. I'd like to be romantic, but I'm generally too oblivious."

All kidding aside, Joshua is a very romantic guy. He loves romance and describes his favorite girls as those who are "beautiful inside and out."

"I'm trying to find the one I want to spend a lot of time with, and that's hard," he says. Now that he's on a successful TV show, he's afraid a girl will date him just because he's an actor. "How am I going to know she'll like me for me?" he asks.

Joshua is the kind of guy who values his privacy. "I really do try and keep this part of my life private," he says. "It's hard, but I'm trying! Anyway, in case you want to know, I'm very single."

According to Joshua, dating is a lot of fun, but he's really looking forward to sharing his life with one special girl. "I go for someone who has her life together," he says. "Someone with her own interests who wouldn't just hang around a movie set with me. I'm looking for someone who's real . . . just real."

Katie Holmes

On *Dawson's Creek,* Katie's character has a major crush on Dawson, her best pal since childhood. To Joey, Dawson is the ideal guy—tall, blond, and handsome. Katie can understand Joey's crush on Dawson because she thinks the world of James, the actor who portrays him.

Katie admits that living on her own can be scary sometimes and it would be great to have someone waiting for her at home. She says the key to true love is being loyal to the person you're going out with. Katie adds that she prefers spending quiet time at home to going to parties.

"I'm a private person," she explains. "I'm not a big socializer. I'm a little shy, but I'm also friendly. And those are the same qualities I look for in a guy."

Cast members say that Katie does have a special guy in her life. But the ultraprivate actress won't reveal his name. All she says is, "My boyfriend and I are extremely close.

We try to spend as much time together as we can."

Whether or not Katie's current beau will be her lifelong mate remains to be seen. "I do know that I definitely want to get married," she says. "And I know it will happen to me when I least expect it."

The Fab Four's Vital Stats

Get to know James!

Name: James Van Der Beek, Jr.

Birthdate: March 8, 1977

Birthplace: Cheshire, Connecticut

Family: Dad, James senior, is a cellular phone executive; Mom, Melinda, runs a gymnastics studio. James has two younger siblings.

Education: Cheshire Academy in Cheshire, Connecticut. James is currently on a leave of absence from Drew University in Madison, New Jersey. His major is English, his minor sociology.

Height: 5′ 10″

Weight: 145 lbs.

Hair color: Dark blond

Eye color: Hazel

Theater credits: James started in school plays and at the Cheshire Theater Ensemble in Connecticut. His theater credits include Danny Zuko in *Grease*, Matt in *The Fantastics*, Lamar/Jeffrey in *Godspell*, the Scarecrow in *The Wizard of Oz*, and Andy Lee in *42nd Street*. He played Fergus in an off-Broadway production of Edward Albee's *Finding the Sun*. In 1994 he played Henry Anderson in the twentieth-anniversary production of the musical *Shenandoah* at the Goodspeed Opera House in East Haddam, Connecticut.

TV credits: *Dawson's Creek;* guest-starred on *The Red Booth Christmas Special* and *Clarissa Explains It All.*

Movie credits: *Angus, I Love You . . . I Love You Not, Harvest*

Ideal girl: "I like honest girls who can carry on a good conversation."

Pet peeve: People who are rude to each other

Favorite school subject: English

Quote: "Hard work is the key to success!"

Favorite sports: "All kinds of sports, especially football!"

Favorite place to relax: The beach

Best qualities: Sincerity and loyalty

How he feels about success: "It's weird to go into a store and pick up a magazine and you're in it."

Biggest influence on his life: "My greatest source of support came from my family. They have backed me all the way."

Tune into Michelle!

Name: Michelle Williams

Birthdate: September 9, 1980

Birthplace: Kalispell, Montana, but her family moved to San Diego when she was nine.

Family: Dad, Larry, is a commodities trader; Mom, Carla, is a homemaker. Michelle has four siblings. She is especially close to her younger sister Paige.

Height: 5′ 3″

Weight: 100 lbs.

Hair color: Blond

Eye color: Hazel

TV credits: *Dawson's Creek;* guest-starred on *Baywatch, Step by Step, Home Improvement.* She also appeared in two unsold pilots for NBC: *Raising Caines* and *In Your Dreams.*

TV movie credits: *A Mother's Justice*

Movie credits: *Lassie, Time Masters, Ethnic Harmony, Species, A Thousand Acres*

First ambition: To be the first female heavyweight champion of the world

Favorite sports: Boxing, running

Favorite snack: Brownies

Favorite lipstick color: Light shades of red or pink

Favorite clothes: Simple, tailored clothes, anything comfortable. "I love pajamas," she says.

Best advice she ever received: "My parents

taught me to follow through with what you start or don't do it all."

Her feelings on fans: "I like being recognized. I think it's great when people come up and ask for my autograph."

Self-description: Independent, determined

Goals: To continue on *Dawson's Creek* and to keep working on new projects

Spotlight on Joshua!

Name: Joshua Jackson

Birthdate: June 11, 1978

Birthplace: Vancouver, British Columbia

Family: His mom is a casting director. His parents are divorced. He has one younger sister.

Current residence: He divides his time between Vancouver and California.

Height: 5' 11"

Weight: 155 lbs.

Hair color: Brown

Eye color: Brown

First acting break: At age nine, he appeared in a series of commercials for British Columbia Tourism.

TV credits: *Dawson's Creek*. Guest-starred on *MacGyver* and *The Outer Limits*. Recurring role on short-lived TV series *Champs*.

TV movie credits: *Robin of Loxley, Ronnie and Julie*

Theater credit: He played Charlie Bucket in a Seattle-based musical production of *Willy Wonka and the Chocolate Factory*.

Movie credits: *Crooked Hearts, The Mighty Ducks, Andre, Digger, Magic in the Water, Tombstone, D2: The Mighty Ducks, D3: The Mighty Ducks, Apt Pupil*

Hobbies: He reads philosophy books in his spare time.

Ideal girl: Someone who is beautiful inside and out

Biggest thrill: Finding out he got the part on *Dawson's Creek*

Self-description: "I'm the class clown!"

His feelings on fans: "It's really nice when fans come up to me just to say hello."

A Closer Look at Katie!

Name: Katherine Holmes

Nickname: Katie

Birthdate: December 18, 1978

Birthplace: Toledo, Ohio

Height: 5'5"

Weight: 108 lbs.

Hair color: Brown

Eye color: Brown

Family: Her father is a lawyer, her mother a homemaker. Katie has four older siblings.

Current residence: She divides her time between Toledo, Ohio, and Los Angeles.

Theater credits: She played the lead role of

Lola in her high school's production of the musical *Damn Yankees*.

TV credits: *Dawson's Creek*

Movie credits: *The Ice Storm, Disturbing Behavior*

Self-description: "I can be serious but I love to have fun."

Favorite way to spend free time: Reading, listening to music

Her feelings on fans: "It feels great to get letters, but I can't believe that people look up to me."

Favorite clothes: Short skirts, pants with short, cropped tops

Favorite foods: Chicken, fresh vegetables

Big secret: "I'm not the easiest person to live with. I'm kind of a slob."

Goals: She wants to continue on *Dawson's Creek,* work on movies, and go to college.

Did You Know . . . ?

James says he is very similar to his onscreen character. "Like Dawson, I wasn't cool," admits the gorgeous blond star. "I played sports and I also did theater. The two worlds didn't exactly overlap."

Michelle's favorite authors are Hermann Hesse, Dostoyevsky, and Kurt Vonnegut, Jr.

Joshua treats himself to one big indulgence per job. When he finished filming *D3: The Mighty Ducks,* he bought himself two big stereo speakers to add on to his stereo. "The next thing I'm going to buy is a nice big-screen TV," he says.

"I got carded when I tried to see *Scream 2,*" says nineteen-year-old Katie, who can easily pass for her *Dawson's Creek* character's age, fifteen. "I'm just glad I brought my ID."

James feels the worst part of being an actor is "losing my privacy and personal time."

Joshua used to read only books by Charles Dickens but now considers *History of Western Philosophy* his "own personal Bible."

When she isn't working on *Dawson's Creek,* Katie likes to go back home to Ohio and spend quality time with her family and friends.

James says the most meaningful show to him while he was growing up was *The Wonder Years.* "I was really into that show," he says.

Katie's character, Joey, is often seen rowing back and forth across the creek between her waterfront shack and Dawson's house. But according to Katie, "I'm not really rowing. They put a rope under the boat and pull it."

Joshua calls James Captain America.

Since Katie is living on her own for the first time, James and Joshua consider her an easy target for practical jokes. "They always say things to get a rise out of me," says Katie. "Very outlandish things, and they succeed."

Michelle says, "A lot of people tell me I look like Jewel and Traci Lords."

James says of his TV role, "I've never played myself before. Dawson is kind of a different take on me at fifteen."

"I've got a vicious independent streak. I love being on my own," says Michelle.

When a reporter asked James the unconventional question "Who is your favorite Beatle?" he had to think for a minute. "I'd have to say Paul," he said. Then, after a pause, he added with a grin, "Actually, it's the drummer who left before they became famous."

Michelle loves New York City. "It is absolutely amazing," she says.

The cast enjoys chilling out together when not working on the show. "We do hang out," says James. "It's kinda sad—you'd think we'd get sick of each other."

Cast and Credits

Cast

Dawson Leery	James Van Der Beek
Jennifer Lindley	Michelle Williams
Pacey Witter	Joshua Jackson
Joey Potter	Katie Holmes
Gail Leery	Mary-Margaret Humes
Mitch Leery	John Wesley Shipp
Bessie Potter	Nina Repeta
Bodie	Obi Ndefo
Grams	Mary Beth Peil

Guest stars: Dylan Neal (Deputy Doug Witter), Leann Hunley (Tamara Jacobs), Ian Bohen (Anderson Crawford), Chris Berry (Eric), Chris Blackwelder (Roger), Eion Bailey (Jen's ex-boyfriend)

Credits

Created by: Kevin Williamson
Executive Producers: Kevin Williamson, Paul Stupin, Charles Rosin

Producers: Greg Prange, Jon Harmon Feldman, Steve Miner

Writers: Kevin Williamson, Jon Harmon Feldman, Dana Baratta, Rob Thomas, Joanne Waters

Directors: Steve Miner, Lou Antonio, Michael Uno

Production Designer: John "J.T." Walker

Edited by: Robert L. Sinise, A.C.E.

Director of Photography: Karl Hermann

Composer: Adam Fields

Theme Music Written and Performed by Paula Cole

Wardrobe Provided by J. Crew

Filmed at Screen Gem Studios, Wilmington, North Carolina

Where to Write to the Stars

Do you want to send your favorite *Dawson's Creek* star a note?

Here's the address:

Your Favorite *Dawson's Creek* Star's Name
c/o *Dawson's Creek*
The WB Network
4000 Warner Boulevard
Burbank, CA 91522

The Official *Dawson's Creek* Web Site is:
www.dawsons-creek.com

About the Author

Grace Catalano is the author of four *New York Times* bestsellers: *Leonardo DiCaprio: Modern-Day Romeo, Leonardo: A Scrapbook in Words and Pictures, New Kids on the Block,* and *New Kids on the Block Scrapbook.* Her other books include biographies of LeAnn Rimes, Brad Pitt, Joey Lawrence, Jason Priestley, Paula Abdul, Gloria Estefan, Richard Grieco, Fred Savage, River Phoenix, Alyssa Milano, and Kirk Cameron. She is also the author of *Teen Star Yearbook,* which includes minibiographies of eighty-five celebrities. Grace Catalano has edited numerous magazines, including *Rock Legend, Star Legend, The Movie Times, CountryBeat, Country Style,* and the teen magazine *Dream Guys.* She and her brother, Joseph, wrote and designed *Elvis: A Tenth Anniversary Tribute, Elvis and Priscilla,* and *Country Music's Hottest Stars.*